# Vellum
# Cards

**Mieke van den Akker**
**Loes Hildering**

FORTE PUBLISHERS

# Contents

© 2004 Forte Uitgevers, Utrecht
© 2004 for the translation by the
publisher
Original title: *Vellumkaarten voor
diverse gelegenheden*

ISBN 90 5877 406 6

This is a publication from
Forte Publishers BV
P.O. Box 1394
3500 BJ Utrecht
The Netherlands

For more information about the creative
books available from Forte Uitgevers:
www.forteuitgevers.nl

Final editing: Gina Kors-Lambers,
Steenwijk, the Netherlands
Photography and digital image editing:
Fotografie Gerhard Witteveen,
Apeldoorn, the Netherlands
Cover and inner design:
BADE creatieve communicatie BV,
Baarn, the Netherlands
Translation: Michael Ford, TextCase,
Hilversum, the Netherlands

# Preface

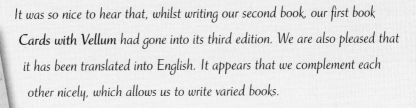

It was so nice to hear that, whilst writing our second book, our first book
**Cards with Vellum** had gone into its third edition. We are also pleased that
it has been translated into English. It appears that we complement each
other nicely, which allows us to write varied books.

In this book, we show you what a wonderful material vellum is to use.
Vellum has so many different possibilities. For example, you can use it
for Lacé cutting, embossing, punching and many other techniques.
Transparent stickers are excellent to use in combination with vellum.
Why don't you try it yourself? You will quickly see that the end result
is fantastic and that the cards are not difficult to make. We wish you lots
of fun with our book.

Mieke van den Akker                    Loes Hildering

# Techniques

## Micro die cuts

The daisy micro die cuts come in packs of four sheets. When you use them, it is easiest to use a soft mat and an embossing stylus. Place the sheet on the mat and push the embossing stylus in the middle of the mat, so that the flower is given the correct shape. A dot or a circle is usually placed in the middle using a leftover piece of a sticker. Therefore, never throw away scrap pieces of stickers, because there is always something they can be used for. The leaf micro die cuts are also supplied in packs. Once the leaves have been pushed out of the sheet, the veins are made using an embossing stylus. This makes them look very natural. You can also fold a leaf double and then put it at an angle through a small ridge machine.

## Gluing vellum

Vellum is stuck to a card using photo glue or double-sided adhesive tape. If you use photo glue, the glue can be seen through the vellum and the vellum will eventually come off of the card. There are rumours that a new, invisible glue for vellum will shortly be available. You can also stick vellum to a card using silicon glue which you can spread out using your fingers. Try it.

## Punching

It is easy to punch vellum using the punch pattern. Copy the pattern and cut it out slightly bigger than the outside line. Stick this in the middle of the vellum and cut the vellum to the same size. Turn the punch upside down and slide the two layers into the punch with the photocopy facing upwards. Next, look for the printed section through the punch and firmly punch the pattern. Do this twelve times. After you finish punching, neatly cut the sheets to size along the outside edge of the punch pattern. Remove the vellum from the copy and you will now have a pretty lace doily.

## Embossing

Emboss parchment paper on a light box. The colour of the parts that you emboss will become lighter.

## Lacé

Vellum is excellent to use for Lacé cutting, because it cuts quite easily. Make sure to always use a sharp knife though.

1. A selection of the materials you will need.

2. It is great to punch squares out of vellum.

3. Embossing and pricking vellum using a stencil.

4. The colours of the cards and the vellum complement each other very well.

Punch pattern

# Materials

- Satin gloss cards
- Aperture cards
- Daisy micro die cuts
- Leaf micro die cuts
- Vellum – Romak (R) and Pergamano (P)
- Frames
- Mica
- Cutting sheets

- Lacé templates
- Various embossing stencils
- Various punches
- Transparent stickers
- Sticker sheets
- Organza ribbon
- Ridge machine
- Prick pen
- Light box

- Embossing stylus
- Soft, red mat
- Scissors
- Ruler
- Knife
- Silicon glue
- Photo glue
- Foam tape
- Double-sided adhesive tape

# Lilac is in!

## Card 1

*Card: lilac with an octagonal aperture • Vellum: lilac roses (R) • Lilac separating sheet • Ivory octagonal frame • Daisy and balloon figure punches • Beech leaf medium punch • Silver beads*

Cut the vellum to size (12 x 12 cm) and use double-sided adhesive tape to stick it against the inside of the card. Place the frame around the opening in the card. Punch three leaves and nine balloons out of lilac paper. Use a pair of scissors to curl six balloons inwards and three balloons outwards. Place a large drop of silicon glue in the middle of the opening in the card and place the six balloons in a circle. Stick the three other balloons in the middle so that it looks like the rose closes slightly. Stick three beads in the middle of the rose. Fold the three leaves double and stick them under the rose. Punch four daisies from lilac paper and four from vellum. Stick them on top of each other in the four corners. Stick a sticker dot in the middle of the daisies.

## Card 2

*Card: lilac • Vellum: lilac roses (R) • Arrow mosaic punch • Lilac Organza ribbon • Gold sticker sheet (943)*

Turn the mosaic punch over and punch a continuous line. Cut a 5 cm wide strip off of the card. Use double-sided adhesive tape to stick the punched border in place. Take the strip you just cut off of the card and stick it on the other side of the card. Cut everything so that it is level with the card. Stick border stickers along the edges. Use double-sided adhesive tape to stick the ribbon on the card. Make a bow and use double-sided adhesive tape to stick it on the ribbon. Stick border stickers at the top and bottom of the card. Stick a text sticker on the card.

## Card 3

*Card: lilac mini square aperture (landscape) • Vellum: lilac roses (R) • Lilac paper • Square mosaic punch • Organza ribbon*

Punch three patterns out of the vellum. Cut them out slightly bigger and use double-sided adhesive tape to stick them behind the openings in the card. Stick some sticker dots or sticker circles in the middle of the patterns.

Cut a piece of vellum (5 x 13 cm) and use double-sided adhesive tape to stick it on the card. Cut a piece of lilac paper (4 x 10 cm) and stick it on the vellum. Cut a piece of lilac ribbon (17 cm) and use double-sided adhesive tape to stick it on the card. Make a bow and use double-sided adhesive tape to stick it on the straight piece of ribbon.

## Card 4

*Card: white satin gloss diamond aperture • White satin gloss daisy micro die cuts • Vellum: lilac roses (R) • Punch pattern • Square mosaic punch • Silver transparent stickers 3101*

Copy the punch pattern and punch the vellum as described in Techniques. Use foam tape to stick the vellum on the card. Push out the micro die cuts and stick them in the middle of the patterns. Stick a square transparent sticker on the vellum and cut it out. Use foam tape to stick the square on the card with one corner facing upwards. Stick sticker circles in the corners. Cut a large flower out of vellum. Stick the flower on a micro die cut and stick this in the middle of the transparent sticker. You can use the small circles from the sticker sheet for the flowers.

# Cards of congratulations

## Card 1

*Card: denim blue square • Vellum: blue decorative swirls (R) • Large and small daisy figure punches • Embossing stencil PR 0561 • Mother-of-pearl beads • Transparent stickers 3102 • Sticker sheet 1033*

Emboss the round pattern and the outside edge in vellum. Cut it out close to the embossed edge. Use photo glue to stick it on the card. Stick a transparent sticker on the vellum and cut it out. Use foam tape to stick it in the middle of the card. Punch three large and three small daisies and use silicon glue to stick them on top of each other. Stick a bead in the middle and use foam tape to stick them on the card. Punch three beech leaves. Shape them and use silicon glue to stick them on the circle. Finish the card with some decorative stickers.

## Card 2

*Card: denim blue mini diamond aperture • Vellum: forget-me-not (R) and blue 1602 (P)*

*• Large and small daisy figure punches • Square mosaic punch • Gold transparent stickers 3101 • Sticker sheets 1033 and 1016*

Punch a pattern out of the forget-me-not vellum and stick a square sticker on it. Place this in the opening in the card and stick a second square sticker on the back. Punch nine small daisies out of the forget-me-not vellum and four large daisies out of the blue vellum. Stick them together as shown in the photograph and use silicon glue to stick everything on the card. Finish the card with some decorative stickers.

## Card 3

*Card: denim blue with three round apertures • Denim blue paper • Vellum: forget-me-not • Butterfly circle punch • Large and small daisy figure punches • Beech leaf punch • Mica • Mother-of-pearl beads • Transparent stickers 3180 • Gold sticker sheet 943 • Decorative text sticker*

Punch three patterns out of the vellum. Cut them out slightly bigger and stick them behind the round openings in the card. Stick transparent stickers on the front of the openings. Finish the back by sticking a piece of mica behind the openings. Punch four small daisies and one large daisy out of vellum and one large daisy out of blue paper. Put the large flower together. Punch three beech leaves out of blue paper and shape them. Stick the leaves under the flower. Stick the small flowers in the middle of the circles and stick beads on them. Use silicon glue to stick everything on

the card. Finish the card with border stickers and a text sticker.

## Card 4

*Card: denim blue • Vellum: forget-me-not (R) and blue 1602 (P) • Quadrant embossing stencil 4602 • Large and small daisy figure punches • Gold sticker sheet 943*

Cut a piece of blue vellum (16 x 9 cm). Use the stencil to emboss the pattern on the left and right-hand sides. Also emboss the edge. Cut it out close to the outside edge and use double-sided adhesive tape to stick it on the card. Repeat this with the forget-me-not vellum (6 x 15 cm) and stick this on top of the blue vellum. Punch four large daisies and four small daisies out of the blue vellum and the forget-me-not vellum. Use silicon glue to stick them together on the card. Decorate the card with border stickers and sticker circles.

# Tulips

## Card 1

*Card: white satin gloss mini diamond aperture • Vellum: light blue decorative swirls (R) • Tulip cutting sheet MD 0104 • Gold transparent stickers 3101 • Gold sticker sheet 1001 • Gold text sticker*

Stick two square stickers on the vellum and cut them out. Cut them diagonally through the middle and stick them on the edges of the card. Stick a piece of vellum behind the opening in the card. Cut out the tulips and use silicon glue to stick them in the middle of the card, making a nice bunch. Stick border stickers around the card.

## Card 2

*Card: white satin gloss square • Vellum: light blue decorative swirls (R) • Tulip cutting sheet MD 0104 • Embossing stencil PG 8802 • Gold sticker sheet 943*

Cut a 4 cm wide strip off of the card. Emboss the vellum and use double-sided adhesive tape to stick it onto the card. Stick a border sticker on the join. Cut out a bunch of tulips and use silicon glue to stick them on the card.

## Card 3

*Card: white satin gloss mini diamond aperture • Satin gloss daisy micro die cuts • Vellum: light blue decorative swirls (R) • Tulip cutting sheet MD 0104 • Ornare template PR 0570 • Gold transparent sticker 3101 • Prick pen • Light box • Embossing stylus*

Stick a transparent sticker on the vellum and cut it out. Stick another transparent sticker in the opening in the card. Place the template in a corner and prick and emboss the pattern. Repeat this in the other corners. Stick a micro die cut on these patterns. Cut out a bunch of tulips and use silicon glue to stick it on the card. Stick sticker dots in the micro die cuts.

## Card 4

*Card: white satin gloss • White satin gloss daisy micro die cuts • Vellum: light blue decorative swirls (R) • Tulip cutting sheet MD 0104 • Quadrant embossing stencil 4602 • Gold transparent sticker 3101 • Gold decorative stickers 1034*

Place the stencil on the card and place it upside down on a light box. Emboss the patterns and the points. Cut the card off along the points. Stick micro die cuts on the points. Cut a piece of vellum (10.5 x 15 cm) and use double-sided adhesive tape to stick it inside the card. Stick a transparent sticker on vellum and cut it out. Use foam tape to stick this square on the card. Cut out a tulip and use silicon glue to stick it on the square. Use photo glue to stick the small squares from the cutting sheet on the card. Stick corner stickers in the corners of the card.

# Sunflowers and daisies

## Card 1

*Card: white satin gloss square • White satin gloss daisy micro die cuts • Vellum: daisies (R) • Mica • Gold sticker sheet 1016 • Gold text sticker*

Cut an 8 cm wide strip off of the card. Use double-

sided adhesive tape to stick mica to the card to make the card complete again. Use double-sided adhesive tape to stick vellum behind the mica. Stick a border sticker along the edge of the card and on the separating line. Push out three different micro die cuts. Stick them on top of each other and then stick them on the left-hand side of the card. Stick another two small micro die cuts on the mica. Stick sticker dots or sticker circles in the middle of the flowers.

## Card 2

*Card: white satin gloss mini square aperture • Vellum: sunflowers (R) • Gold sticker sheets 943, 1034 and 1036 • Gold transparent stickers 3101*

1.

2.

3.

4.

Stick two transparent stickers and two butterflies on the vellum and cut them out. Cut the squares diagonally through the middle and stick them on the card. Fold the wings of the butterflies upwards. Use silicon glue to stick the bodies of the butterflies on the card. Stick a transparent sticker in the opening in the card and another one inside the card. Stick a butterfly on this square. Stick border stickers around the outside of the card. Stick corner stickers in the corners of the card and stick sticker circles on the yellow triangles.

## Card 3

*Card: white satin gloss mini diamond aperture • Vellum: sunflowers (R) • Gold sticker sheets 943, 1013 and 1036 • Gold transparent stickers 3101*
Stick three transparent stickers on the vellum and cut them out. Cut two squares diagonally through the middle and stick them in the correct places on the card. Place the third square in the opening in the card and stick a transparent sticker to the back of it. Stick a butterfly on the vellum. Cut out the butterfly and fold the wings upwards. Stick the

body of the butterfly to the vellum. Stick the squares with the butterflies in the correct place on the card. Stick border stickers around the outside of the card.

## Card 4

*Card: yellow • Satin white daisy micro die cuts • Vellum: sunflowers (R) • Daisy figure punch • Mica • Gold transparent stickers 3101 • Gold sticker sheet 1016*

Cut a 6 cm wide strip off of the card. Use double-sided adhesive tape to stick mica to the card to make the card complete again. Use double-sided adhesive tape to stick vellum behind the mica. Stick three transparent stickers on the vellum and cut them out. Use foam tape to stick them on the left-hand side of the card. Push out three micro die cuts and stick them on the card. Use the figure punch to make three flowers and stick them on the other flowers. Stick border stickers along the edges and the separating line. Stick a text sticker on the card.

# Anniversary

## Card 1

*Card: green satin gloss • Vellum: green 1600 (P)
• Lacé template 50 • Daisy figure punch • Gold
sticker sheets 1016 and 1033*

Use the Lacé template to cut the pattern in the
vellum. Cut a 5.5 cm strip out of the card and
use double-sided adhesive tape to stick the
vellum pattern in the opening. Cut it even with
the edge of the card. Stick a piece of mica
behind the card to give it some strength. Punch
some daisies and use silicon glue to stick them
on the vellum. Decorate the card with border
stickers and corner stickers.

## Card 2

*Card: green satin gloss • Satin gloss paper
• Vellum: turquoise decorative swirls (R)
• Embossing stencils AE 1205, AE 1402 and
PG 8802 • White Organza ribbon • Gold sticker
sheets 1016 and 108*

Emboss the text 3 cm from the edge of the card.
Also emboss the outside edge and cut the card
off along the embossed edge. Use double-sided
adhesive tape to stick a strip of vellum behind
it. Emboss two or more squares from the
template and cut them out. Emboss the initials
in the squares. Place the template with the
letters on the front of the paper to prevent the

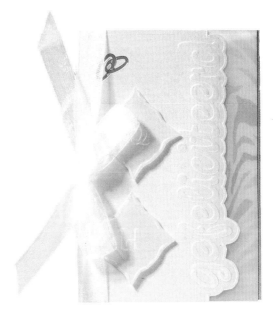

letters being a mirror image. Use foam tape to
stick the squares on the card. Stick a bow at the
bottom of the card.

## Card 3

*Card: green satin gloss • Vellum: turquoise
decorative swirls (R) • Embossing templates
PG 8802 and AE 1201 • Gold sticker sheets
1016, 1033 and 108*

Emboss "Congratulations" diagonally across the card. Also emboss the outside edge and cut the card off along this edge. Emboss some dots. Do this carefully and make sure that the dots are parallel with the edges of the card. Cut a piece of mica to the correct size and use double-sided adhesive tape to stick it inside the card. Cut a piece of vellum to the correct size and stick it behind the mica. Decorate the card with some decorative stickers.

## Card 4

*Card: green satin gloss • Daisy micro die cuts • Satin gloss paper • Vellum: green 1600 (P) • Quadrant embossing stencil 4602 • Large daisy punch • Gold sticker sheets 3180 and 1016*

Emboss the pattern in the left-hand and right-hand sides of the vellum. Also emboss the outside edge and cut the vellum off along this edge. Use double-sided adhesive tape to stick the vellum on the card. Stick two round stickers on satin gloss paper and cut them out. Use foam tape to stick them in the middle of the card. Take six small micro die cuts and two large micro die cuts. Punch two daisies out of the vellum. Stick the small vellum daisies in the large satin gloss daisies and use silicon glue to stick them on the card. Also stick the small daisies on the card.

1.

2.

3.

4.

# Marriage

### Card 1

*Card: white, oval aperture • Satin gloss leaf and daisy micro die cuts*
*• Vellum: gold "Congratulations" (P)*
*• Gold sticker sheets 844, 101 and 108*

Use double-sided adhesive tape to stick vellum (10.5 x 15 cm) behind the opening in the card. Stick a border sticker around the opening. Stick some leaves and some flowers around the opening. Decorate the card with border stickers.

### Card 2

*Card: white satin gloss • White satin gloss daisy micro die cuts • Vellum: silver "Love" (P) • Lacé template 51 • Quadrant embossing stencil 4602 • Mica • Mother-of-pearl beads • Gold sticker sheet 1017*

Cut a 7 cm wide strip out of the front of the card. Emboss the round border on the remaining piece of card and on the piece which was cut off of the card. Take a piece of vellum (10.5 x 10.5 cm) and use the Lacé template to cut the pattern in the middle. Use double-sided adhesive tape to stick it against the back between the embossed pieces. Cut the vellum level with

the edge of the card. Use double-sided adhesive tape to stick a piece of mica behind it to give it some strength. Use silicon glue to stick micro die cuts with beads in the middle of the card.

## Card 3

*Card: white satin gloss • White satin gloss micro die cuts • Vellum: Gold "Congratulations" (P)*
*• Quadrant embossing stencil 4602 • Mica*
*• Gold sticker sheets 108 and 1016*

Cut a 7.5 cm wide strip off of the card and then cut a 4 cm strip off of this. Use double-sided adhesive tape to stick mica (10.5 x 15 cm) between the two pieces of card to make the card complete. Use double-sided adhesive tape to stick vellum behind the mica. Stick the embossed borders on the left and right-hand edges of the card or emboss the card before sticking the mica and the vellum to the card. Use silicon glue to stick eight micro die cuts on the card. Decorate the card with some decorative stickers.

## Card 4

*Card: white, round aperture • Vellum: gold text (P) • Cutting sheet 2228 (Nel van Veen) • Lacé template 13 • White Organza ribbon*

*• Mother-of-pearl beads • Gold sticker sheets 1016 and 1033*

Use the Lacé template to cut a pattern in a piece of vellum which is the same size as the card. Use double-sided adhesive tape to stick the vellum behind the opening in the card. Prick two holes every 2 cm around the opening. Take a piece of Organza ribbon which is 15 cm longer than the circumference of the circle and attach it to the card with three stitches each time. Add a bead with each third stitch. Make sure the ribbon stands up a bit between each set of stitches. Tie the end of the ribbon in a bow. Cut a 3D bouquet of flowers from the cutting sheet. Decorate the card with some decorative stickers.

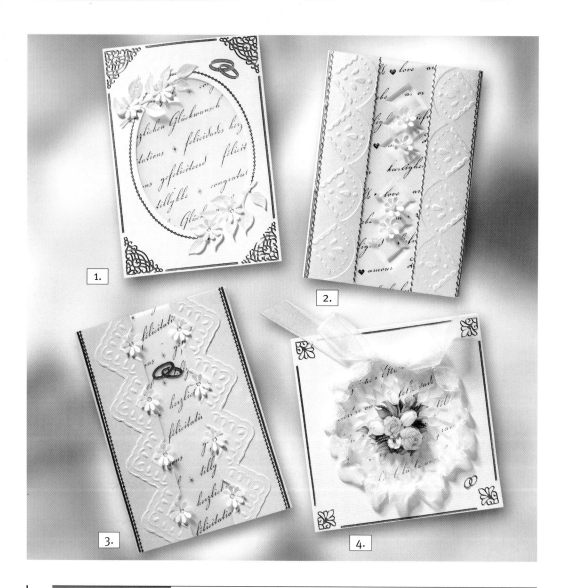

1.

2.

3.

4.

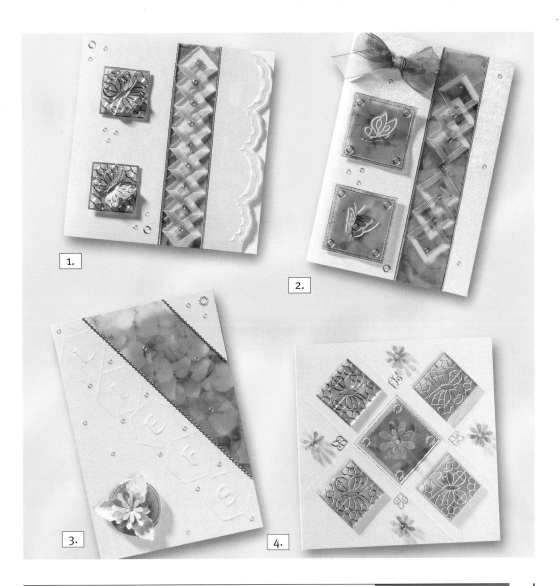

1.

2.

3.

4.

# Get well soon

## Card 1

*Card: pink, satin gloss square • Vellum: red hydrangea (R) • Lacé template 1 • Embossing stencil EE 3401 • Gold sticker sheet 1036*

Use the template to cut the pattern in the vellum. Cut a 6 cm wide strip off of the card and emboss the edge of the piece that you just cut off. Cut this piece to the correct size and use double-sided adhesive tape to stick the Lacé pattern between the separate pieces of card. Stick a piece of mica behind it to give it some strength. Stick four square butterfly stickers on

red vellum. Cut out two squares and use foam tape to stick them on the card. Cut out the other two butterflies, fold them double and use

silicon glue to stick them on the card. Decorate the card with some decorative stickers.

## Card 2

*Card: pink satin gloss • Vellum: red hydrangea (R) • Red Organza ribbon • Lacé template 51 • Mica • Transparent stickers 1031 • Gold sticker sheet 1036*

Use the Lacé template to cut the pattern in a piece of vellum (7.5 x 10.5 cm). Cut a 5 cm wide strip out of the card and use double-sided adhesive tape to stick the vellum between the separate pieces of card. Cut the vellum at the bottom so that it is level with the card. Stick a piece of mica behind the vellum to give it some strength. Stick two transparent stickers on vellum and cut them out. Also stick two butterflies on vellum and cut them out. Stick a piece of mica behind the vellum to strengthen it. Use foam tape to stick the square stickers on the card and use silicon glue to stick the butterflies on the squares. Use silicon glue to stick the bow on the card. Decorate the card with sticker circles and border stickers.

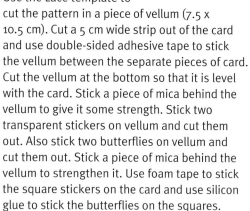

## Card 3

*Card: pink satin gloss • Daisy and leaf micro die cuts • Vellum: red hydrangea (R) • Embossing stencil AB 1402 • Gold sticker sheet 1016 • Transparent stickers 3180*

Decide in advance which text and how many letters you wish to use. Determine the location of the embossed hexagons. First, emboss the hexagons and then emboss the letters in the hexagons. Remember that the stencil must be placed on the front of the card, otherwise the letters will be a mirror image in the hexagons. Cut the card diagonally, 3 cm from the top left-hand corner to 3 cm from the bottom right-hand corner.

Use double-sided adhesive tape to stick a piece of vellum (10.5 x 15 cm) to the inside of the card. Cut off the top right-hand corner of the card which was cut off and stick it in the corner of the vellum. Stick a round transparent sticker on the vellum and cut it out. Take two different daisy micro die cuts and use silicon glue to stick them together. Use silicon glue to stick three leaves under the daisy. Decorate the card with sticker circles.

## Card 4

*Card: pink satin gloss mini square aperture • Vellum: red hydrangea (R) • Large and small daisy figure punches • Gold sticker sheets 1036 and 1033 • transparent stickers 1031*

Stick butterfly stickers and transparent stickers on the vellum and cut them out. Place the transparent sticker in the opening in the card and stick a second sticker to the back of it. Use foam tape to stick the four butterfly stickers on the card. Punch five small daisies and a large daisy out of the vellum. Use silicon glue to stick one small daisy in the large daisy and then stick all the daisies on the card. Decorate the card with sticker circles and corner stickers.

# Christmas

## Card 1

*Card: olive green square with a round aperture*
*• Red leaf micro die cuts • Vellum: green*
*mother-of-pearl (R) • Thin olive green paper*
*• Round ivory frame • Gold sticker sheets 1034,*
*364 and 1030*

Stick green vellum behind the opening in the card. Stick olive green paper to the back of the vellum. Stick the round frame on the front of the card. Push out the leaves, fold them double and put them through a ridge machine. Stick them on the frame. Stick bells on vellum. Cut them out and use foam tape to stick them on the vellum in the opening. Stick stickers in the corners of the card and use border stickers to join them together. Stick stars and a text sticker on the card.

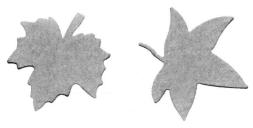

## Card 2

*Card: olive green card with three square apertures*
*• Thin red paper • Vellum: green 1600 (P) • Olive*

*green paper • Ivory paper with a Christmas print*
*(R) • Christmas tree multi frame punch • Green*
*Organza ribbon • Gold transparent stickers 3106*
*and 1018 • Gold sticker sheet 1016*

Punch three patterns in the vellum. Cut them out slightly bigger and stick them behind the openings in the card. Stick transparent stickers on them. Stick red paper (10.5 x 15 cm) to the inside of the card. Stick a label sticker on the text and cut it out. Stick everything on a piece of olive green paper and cut it out slightly bigger to give a small green border. Decorate the card with border stickers and stars. Make a hole in the card. Thread the ribbon through the hole and tie a bow on the label.

## Card 3

*Card: olive green card with three round apertures • Vellum: green 1600 (P) • Thin red paper • Tree window circle punch • Red Organza ribbon • Gold sticker sheets 1016 and 3180*

Punch three patterns out of vellum and stick them behind the openings in the card. Stick round stickers on the vellum. Stick red paper (10.5 x 15 cm) inside the card. Tie a bow and use silicon glue to stick it on the card. Decorate the card with border stickers and stars.

## Card 4

*Card: olive green card with three square apertures • Red leaf micro die cuts • Vellum: green mother-of-pearl • Arrow mosaic punch • Star border punch • Gold sticker sheets 1016 and 264*

Punch three patterns in the green vellum. Cut them out slightly bigger and use double-sided adhesive tape to stick them behind the openings in the card. Use the border punch to punch two borders which are as long as the card. Use photo glue to stick them on the card. Stick border stickers along the punched borders. Push out two branches and use an embossing stylus and a soft mat to scratch veins in the leaves. Use small drops of silicon glue to stick the branches between the borders. Stick the text sticker between the branches. Stick circle stickers on the patterns.

# Cards on the cover *(photograph on page 32)*

## Card 1

*Card: blue satin gloss square • Blue satin gloss daisy and leaf micro die cuts • Vellum: light blue decorative swirls (R) • Sunflower border punch (Fiskars) • Flower jumbo picture punch • Silver sticker sheet 943*

Use the border punch to punch a border out of vellum. Cut a 2 cm wide strip off of the card. Use double-sided adhesive tape to stick the punched border onto the card. Stick the strip you cut off behind the vellum. Punch a flower out of the vellum. Stick the flower in the middle of the card. Use an embossing stylus and a soft mat to push out the flower and leaf micro die cuts and stick them on the card. Stick border stickers on the card. Decorate the card with circle stickers.

## Card 2

*Card: blue satin gloss square • Blue satin gloss daisy micro die cuts • Blue satin gloss paper • Vellum: light blue decorative swirls (R) • Flower photo corner figure punch • Silver sticker sheet 943*

Punch out the corners of the card using the figure punch. Cut the vellum so that it fits exactly between the photo corners. Stick border stickers around the card. Punch the shape out of the blue satin gloss paper and use foam tape to stick it in the middle of the card. Stick three large micro die cuts on this shape and then stick three small micro die cuts on top. Stick four double micro die cuts around this shape. Decorate the card with sticker dots and circle stickers.

## Card 3

*Card: blue satin gloss • Satin gloss paper • Vellum: blue decorative swirls (R) • Large and small daisy figure punches • Beech leaf punch • Flower border punch • Bite punch • White Organza ribbon • Mother-of-pearl beads • Transparent stickers 3102*

Cut a piece of vellum (10.5 x 15 cm). Use the border punch to punch three sides. Fold 4 cm of the top of the vellum over and fold this over the top of the card. Use double-sided adhesive tape to stick the short piece of vellum to the back of the card. Stick a transparent sticker on the vellum and cut it out. Punch three large daisies out of satin gloss paper, and three large daisies and three small daisies out of vellum. Stick the flowers together and punch three beech leaves. Stick the three flowers on the circle and use silicon glue to stick the leaves underneath. Tie a bow and use silicon glue to stick it on the card.

*Thanks to Romak for providing the materials. Shopkeepers can order the materials from: Romak in Hillegom, the Netherlands, and Kars en Co B.V. in Ochten, the Netherlands.*

The Spirelli punch, the Pigo stencil and the Ornare template can be ordered from Avec in Waalwijk, the Netherlands. The Jumbo punch and the small ridge machine can be ordered from Vaessen in Nuth, the Netherlands.